Wild Clematis

Yarrow

Silverweed

Ivy

Acer

Blackberry

Herb Robert

Pressed Flower Designs

Phyllis Walker

Lutterworth Press
Cambridge

Lutterworth Press
P.O. Box 60
Cambridge CB1 2NT

British Library Cataloguing in Publication Data

Walker, Phyllis
    Pressed flower designs.
    1. Pressed flower pictures
    I. Title
    745.92'8   SB449.3.P7
    ISBN 0-7188-2629-9

First published in 1988 by Lutterworth Press

Printed in Singapore

Contents

Acknowledgements

Enduring thanks to my husband Alan for his constant interest, support and encouragement.

I am indebted to Tony and Pat Wing of Stoke Gallery, Gosport for their friendly interest and professional expertise in mounting and heat sealing all my work.

Thanks are also due to West Dean College, West Dean, Chichester, where I learnt so much and received such inspiration in the craft classes I attended there.

Introduction

I have always taken delight in lavender bags, dried flowers and pot-pourri but it was only recently that I discovered the special delights of pressed flowers.

Many wild flowers press well. I find wayside and hedgerow provide a great variety of suitable material. Vigorous young specimens of buttercups, daisies, cow parsley, leaves and grasses are abundant. Small grey-backed leaves of the rampant bramble are everywhere. New shoots of wild clematis (old man's beard) festoon the springtime hedges and summer brings trails of honeysuckle. I use all these lovely things. Now that many seedsmen stock wild plant seeds some protected favourites can be grown in the garden. The dainty leaves of Herb Robert are the first to appear in mine.

My garden is attractive in spring. Small displays of violets, daffodils, tulips, grape-hyacinths and early stocks are colourful but not ideal for pressing. They are left to run their flowery course. Some other spring flowers can be pressed but summer is my peak pressing time. Flowers are gathered at their best, on fine dry days free of early dew and damp. These are carefully prepared and placed in the flower press as soon as possible.

Using these flowers is absorbing and rewarding. The designs on the following pages are reproduced to original size and reflect my preference and interest in smaller flowers. Colour retention is good, they press well and are excellent for book markers, greetings cards and pictures. These delighted the Victorians and are popular again today. Colour may change in time but the appeal of the design remains.

Pressed Flower

Designs

for

pictures and

cards

Lobelia

Lobelia is available in many shades but the deep blue flower gives the best results. "Sapphire", the trailing variety with the white eye, fine stems and buds is most effective and lovely to use.

The oval design has an inner pink mount matching the larkspur. Delphiniums echo the blue of the lobelia. Miniature rosebuds, wild clematis leaves and spikes of dark heuchera complete the arrangement.

Heartsease

This tiny pansy has many names but the most popular is Heartsease. It flowers in abundance, seeds and germinates freely. Flower, stem and small leaves are pressed separately.

In the language of flowers
pansies are for thoughts.

Catmint

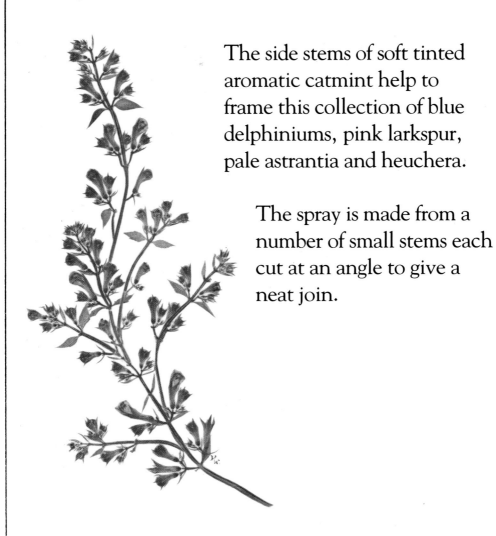

The side stems of soft tinted aromatic catmint help to frame this collection of blue delphiniums, pink larkspur, pale astrantia and heuchera.

The spray is made from a number of small stems each cut at an angle to give a neat join.

Heather

White heather from a bouquet makes a pretty keepsake. It can also be used to convey a 'Good Luck' message for special occasions. To avoid a thick heavy look, woody stems must be pared down and some of the tiny florets removed before pressing.

Heuchera

This compact perennial in shades of pink and carmine is a favourite. It has good colour retention and in this design is used with pink larkspur, delphiniums, three green-tipped astrantia and yellow wild trefoil.

Blue for a boy . . .

A combination of garden and wild
flowers to greet the new born.
Three delphiniums, surrounded by
buds and flowers of lobelia,
stitchwort and wild clematis leaves.

. . . *Pink for a girl*

Clear pink larkspur is matched
with heuchera in company with
the wild stitchwort and tiny
clematis leaves.

Passiontide

Sections of pale lime green
acer leaves and buds of
larkspur make a suitable
frame for the striking
purple of the
flowers – a
traditional
Passiontide
colour.

Japanese Anemone

When pressed it is the underside of the flower that has most appeal. In this design flowers have been used in this way and given a centre of kingcup stamens. The two small flowers gain interest from the addition of acer leaf sections and wild nipplewort.

Astrantia or Hattie's Pincushion

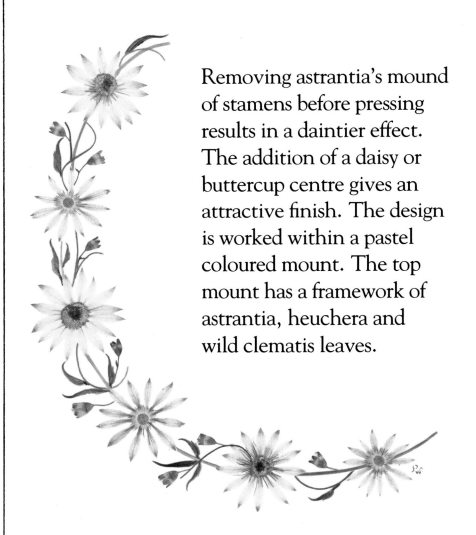

Removing astrantia's mound of stamens before pressing results in a daintier effect. The addition of a daisy or buttercup centre gives an attractive finish. The design is worked within a pastel coloured mount. The top mount has a framework of astrantia, heuchera and wild clematis leaves.

Hellebore-green . . .

This attractive plant, known also as Christmas
Rose, is a welcome sight in winter. The
lime and green flowers are unusual
and only stamens and seeds decorate
this trio. The single flower
shown with small clematis
leaves has the seeded centre
replaced by kingcup
stamens.

. . . and Hellebore-pink

The Lenten Rose – as the name
suggests, flowers a little later.
Petals are suffused with green
and rose pink. Best picked
before stamens coarsen.

Spring Posy

These posies include florets of yellow oxlip, mauve denticulata, deep toned polyanthus and azaleas with distinctive stamens. Colour is enhanced by placing two florets together.

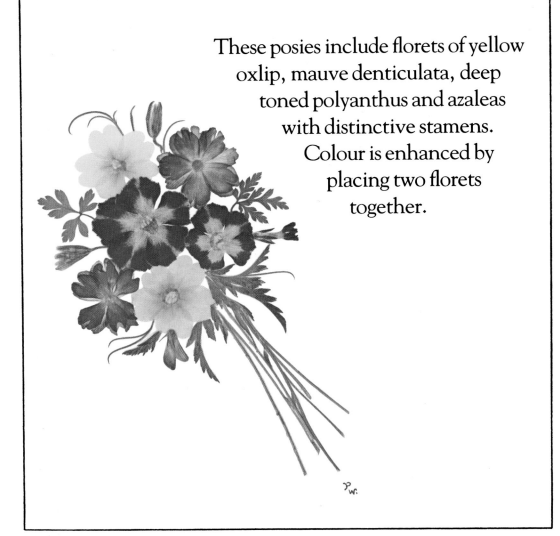

Miniature Rosebuds

Miniature rosebuds grow about ten inches high and are very hardy. Buds press well. With a sharp knife halve the rosebud and stem from top to bottom. This will reduce bulk and retain shape.

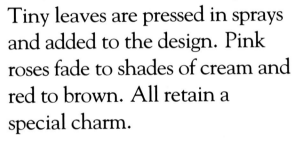

Tiny leaves are pressed in sprays and added to the design. Pink roses fade to shades of cream and red to brown. All retain a special charm.

Corydalis

Corydalis is at home in the rockery, seeds freely and appears in nooks and crannies around the  garden. It makes an interesting colour combination with pale pink heuchera. Whole stems have been pressed and the design kept simple. Where stems appear to cross they have been cut and rejoined in line with the stem.

Larkspur

This popular garden flower grows
easily from seed and comes in
pretty shades of mauve and
pink. Small buds press
well and are included in
this design with tiny
pink heuchera and
lobelia.

Viola

Violas – smaller than pansies but just as pretty – need dainty flowers to accompany them. Here, stems of cream dropwort and pink heuchera are used. Violas with well defined faces give the best results.

Acer Leaves

These lovely serrated leaves in a
range of russet tones make a
very attractive composition.
Here the fluid lines of this
specimen suggested the
star shaped pattern,
assembled from leaf
sections.

Virginia Creeper

These leaves, picked green, later
turn to chestnut brown. They
are dominated by the many
tendrils that flow and twist
in all directions and
highlight the picture.
An interesting subject
for a large design.
Stems are pressed
complete.

47

Grasses from Near . . .

Highways and byways abound with lovely green grasses suitable for pressing but all must be picked young before the seed matures. Green ferns or fronds of bracken will later turn to a pleasing brown.

It helps the design if stems have been encouraged to curve.

. . . *and Far*

Dry grasses are easy travellers and
are reminders of happy holidays.
Picked for their golden colouring
and interesting form and dried
naturally by the sun, they
need a comparatively
short time in the
press.

Bookmarkers and Gift Tags

These small items appeal to all ages. Their attraction lies in the simplicity or detail of the design. Even a single flower or leaf is pleasing when used on this scale. This is an ideal way to use specimens in short supply.

Flowers
from the
Wayside
and
Hedgerow

Cow Parsley

The wild and dainty cow parsley decorates much of our wayside in April, May and June. Side stems with their specimens of smaller flowers are pressed as one. Seedheads show off their structure to complete the picture.

Buttercup

Buttercups evoke pleasant memories of childhood and summer days. They are at their best when used in a simple and natural display. Field buttercups have the finer stems and their smaller buds soften the line of the design.

Daisies

Daisies are simple and charming.
On greeting cards they have a nostalgic
appeal. Pick pink tipped flowers for effect
and press them separately from their
stems.

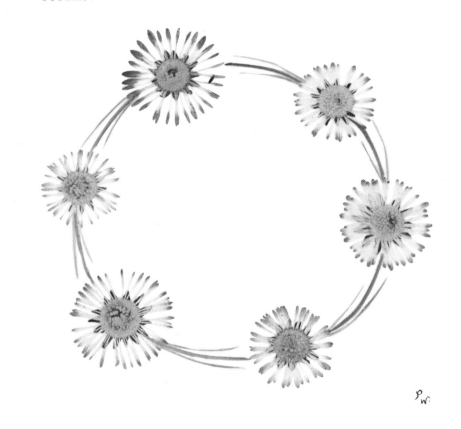

Honeysuckle

The sweet smelling woodbine flowers in midsummer. The flowerhead is gently taken apart and buds and trumpets pressed separately. Leaves should be small, twiggy stems young and all re-assembled in natural form. Flowers and leaves darken in time and remain very attractive.

Dog Rose or Sweet Briar

To prepare rosebuds for pressing cut in half vertically through bud and calyx. Remove surplus petals leaving just enough to retain form. With single-open roses, cut away calyx and press entire rose. Woody stems are reduced by cutting lengthwise or paring with a sharp knife. This is not difficult and is essential for successful results.

Wild Carrot

The first flowers of the season are three or more inches across but later the side stems produce smaller specimens which press beautifully. Their lacelike patterned structure makes it possible to use either side of the flower very effectively. Stems are coarse and some must be whittled down.

Flowers of the Hedge

Roses and honeysuckle, which in summer shared
the same garden hedge and scented the night air
still complement each other.

"So doth the woodbine the sweet honeysuckle
Gently entwist."
                                        Shakespeare

Bramble leaves keep company with young honeysuckle

Variations on a Theme

Larkspur, delphiniums, heuchera and lobelia make a popular combination of colour and form.

The following pages show a variety of ways in which they can be used for greeting cards and pictures.

76

Wild Carrot

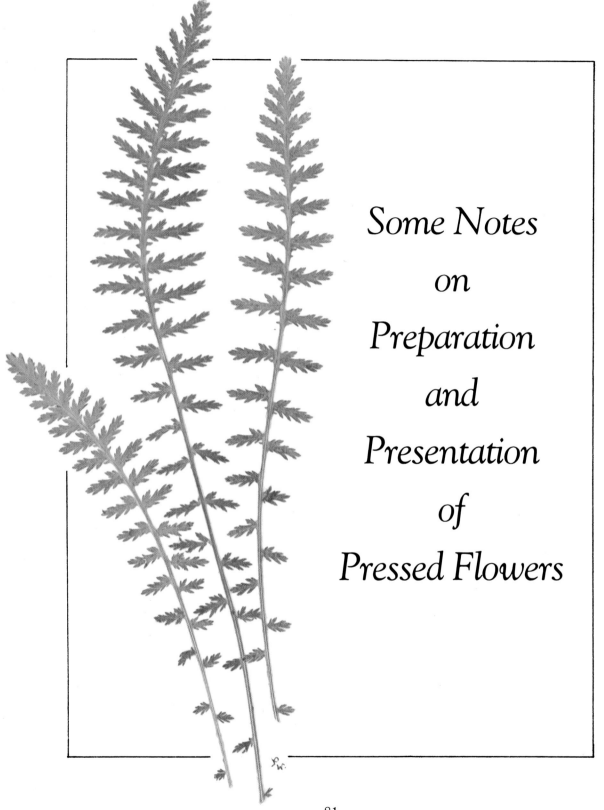

Some Notes
on
Preparation
and
Presentation
of
Pressed Flowers

Useful Materials

1. If a flower press is not available, good results are obtained when flowers are placed between sheets of blotting paper, layered with strawboard and weighted with heavy books or wrapped bricks. Old telephone directories give successful results if pages are interleaved with blotting paper at intervals and weighted.

2. Fine pointed tweezers are invaluable for handling pressed flowers.

3. Small scissors.

4. Copydex – a latex adhesive – is best used in small amounts from a plastic lid.

5. A fine pointed plastic knitting needle or the similar end of a paintbrush can be used to apply adhesive and is easily wiped clean.

6. Plain greetings cards and mounting card are available from good suppliers of art materials.

7. Transpaseal – a light, self adhesive plastic film, finishes, seals and protects cards and bookmarkers.

Framed flower pictures must be in direct contact with the glass to exclude air.

Heat sealing, available at many galleries, gives an excellent finish to flower pictures. All the designs in this book have been heat sealed.

Do:

- pick flowers under dry conditions.
- press flowers as soon as possible after picking.
- press stems separately and encourage them to curve.
- reduce woody stems by paring.
- remove surplus stamens, leaves and buds before pressing.
- take care that petals placed between sheets of blotting paper are as flat as possible.
- leave material undisturbed in the press for at least six weeks before using.
- store your press in dry, airy conditions.

Do:

- spend time in arranging designs.
- use adhesive sparingly – only minute spots are required.
- limit the material in any one design – too little is better than too much.
- cut and rejoin stems to give continuity of line where necessary.
- consider tinted mounts when having work framed – it can enhance a design.
- hang pressed flower work away from bright sunlight to avoid undue fading.
- experiment with a few new flowers each season and note the results.

Don't:

- use corrugated card in the press. It has a bruising effect on the petals. Strawboard gives good results.
- overcrowd flowers when pressing. They need space for drying out.
- waste valuable space by pressing unsuitable flowers e.g. overlarge specimens.
- overlook the need to name-tag pages so that flowers can be located when required.
- forget the importance of space in showing some specimens to advantage.
- overlap flowers or stems as the result is disappointing.

Don't:

- use flowers or leaves that are not well pressed – the finished work will not be pleasing.
- discard flowers that are fragile after pressing. Detached petals can be replaced and flowers mended.
- throw away damaged, unused flowers. Added to pot-pourri they give colour and interest.

- hurry over work. Good designs are time consuming, enjoyable and worthwhile.

Index

For identification purposes flowers and leaves are indexed once.

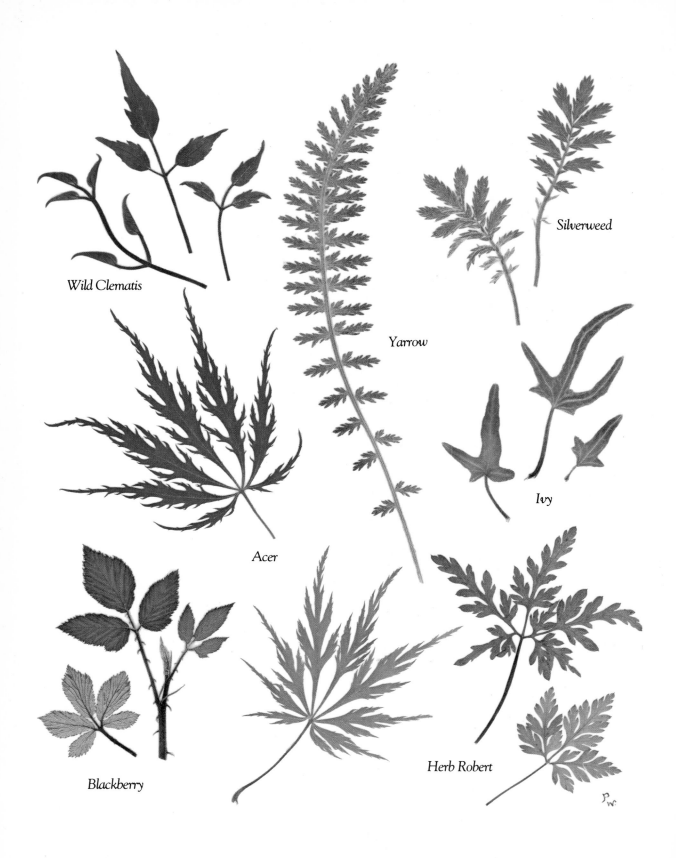

Wild Clematis

Silverweed

Yarrow

Acer

Ivy

Blackberry

Herb Robert